**ACPL ITEM
DISCARDED**

DO NOT REMOVE
CARDS FROM POCKET

Books in This Series

Better Archery for Boys and Girls
Better Baseball for Boys
Better Basketball for Boys
Better Basketball for Girls
Better Bicycling for Boys and Girls
Better Bowling for Boys
Better Boxing for Boys
Better Camping for Boys
Better Field Hockey for Girls
Better Football for Boys
Better Golf for Boys
Better Gymnastics for Boys
Better Gymnastics for Girls
Better Horseback Riding for Boys and Girls
Better Ice Hockey for Boys
Better Ice Skating for Boys and Girls
Better Karate for Boys
Better Kite Flying for Boys and Girls
Better Physical Fitness for Boys
Better Physical Fitness for Girls
Better Roller Skating for Boys and Girls
Better Skateboarding for Boys and Girls
Better Soccer for Boys and Girls
Better Softball for Boys and Girls
Better Surfing for Boys
Better Swimming and Diving for Boys and Girls
Better Synchronized Swimming for Girls
Better Table Tennis for Boys and Girls

Better Tennis for Boys and Girls
Better Track and Field Events for Boys
Better Track for Girls
Better Volleyball for Girls
Better Water Skiing for Boys

BETTER FIELD HOCKEY
for Girls

George Sullivan

DODD, MEAD & COMPANY · NEW YORK

PICTURE CREDITS

Smith College Archives, 8; U.S. Field Hockey Association, 10; Wellesley College, 9. All other photographs are by George Sullivan.

1 2 3 4 5 6 7 8 9 10

Library of Congress Cataloging in Publication Data

Sullivan, George, 1927–
    Better field hockey for girls.

    SUMMARY: Tactics and techniques of field hockey, an American sport in which women are more dominant than men.
    1. Field hockey—Juvenile literature. 2. Sports for women—Juvenile literature. [1. Field hockey] I. Title.
GV1017.H7S9   796.35′5   81–2747
ISBN 0–396–07970–9   AACR2

2145671

The author is grateful to the many people who helped him in the preparation of this book, providing background information and photographs. These include Sandra F. Vanderstoep, U.S. Field Hockey Association; Linda Carroll, Fordham University; Jen Shillingford, Bryn Mawr College; Tim Sullivan; Herb Field, Herb Field Art Studio; Gary Wagner, Wagner-International Photos; Bill Sullivan and Aime LaMontagne.

Special thanks are offered Darlene Wollson, coach of the girls' field hockey team at West Springfield High School, West Springfield, Massachusetts; Sahler Smith, Athletic Director, and these members of the team who posed for photographs: Mary Lynn Green, Terry Dunn, Liz Campanini, Lisa Camp, Kathy Owen, Andrea Burns, Kim Zacharie, Jessica Dobie, Marie Mangini, Pam Beals, Joanne Mahoney, Donna O'Brien, Amy Willey, Lori Camp, Evie Sakowicz, Lisa Kosior, and Jill Shields.

CONTENTS

Field hockey at Smith College in the early 1900s.

THE WOMAN'S SPORT

Field hockey, said to be the oldest of all stick-and-ball games, was long considered too rough a sport for women. Only men played it.

That situation didn't begin to change until 1887 when women in England began playing field hockey for the first time. The sport began to take root in the United States not long after. Late in August, 1901, Constance M. K. Applebee of the British College of Physical Education demonstrated the game for a group of curious observers in a small concrete courtyard outside the Harvard University gymnasium in Cambridge, Massachusetts.

She later taught the sport at several women's colleges in the northeastern United States—Vassar, Wellesley, Mount Holyoke, Bryn Mawr, and Smith.

In 1922, as interest continued to build, a group of enthusiastic players and coaches formed the United States Field Hockey Association, which serves as the governing body for the sport for women. (Men's field hockey is governed by the Field Hockey Association of America.) The U.S. Field Hockey Association supervises the sport on a school, club, and college level, produces films about the game, sponsors coaching clinics, issues the sport's official rules, and conducts sectional and national tournaments.

The International Federation of Women's Field Hockey Associations was formed in 1927, with the U.S. Field Hockey Association as one of its members. Today, about 35 countries belong to the Federation.

Field hockey is one American sport in which women are more dominant than men. And it has never been more popular. Women's varsity programs are underway in some 2,000 high schools and 400 colleges. More than 500 field hockey clubs are organized for local, regional, and national competition.

Most players represent the states of Pennsylvania, New York, New Jersey, California, Massachusetts, Connecticut, and Maryland. Teams are also active in Missouri, Ohio, Michigan, and Virginia.

Part of field hockey's increasing popularity stems from the growth of women's sports in general during the 1970s and 1980s. Women's field hockey was named an official Olympic sport in 1980, and that was a factor in attracting new players and fans.

The game has gone through a period of enormous change in recent years. American teams used to be known for a "hit-ahead-and-chase" style of play.

Wellesley College field hockey, also in the early 1900s.

Chris Larson (left) and Karen Shelton (center) starred for U.S. Olympic Field Hockey Team, ranked third in the world in 1980.

But not anymore. Now the emphasis is on teamwork, on controlling the ball with quick and accurate passes and clever dribbling. Tactical planning is also the order of the day.

The women's field hockey team that represented the United States in 1980, perhaps the best American team up to that time, typified this "new" thinking. It was the first American team to win an international tournament, taking first place in the Ireland Tournament of Dublin early in 1980.

Later that year, on the basis of its showing in a 14-game, 19-day tour throughout Europe, the American team captured one of the six qualifying berths in the Olympic Games.

Because of America's boycott of the Games that year, one can only speculate on how the U.S. team might have fared in Olympic competition. But if future U.S. teams show the same skill and determination as the 1980 team, American field hockey players may one day be ranked as the world's best.

HOW THE GAME IS PLAYED

Field hockey is a game played on a rectangular field between two teams of eleven players. Using long, hooked sticks, they compete in driving a small ball into each other's goal. It is a game of constant movement, with play surging up and down the field. While there are few set plays, players respond to various game situations with well-planned strategy and tactics.

The field is about the size of a football field—100 yards (91 meters) long and 60 yards (55 meters) wide.

Three parallel lines spaced 25 yards apart separate the length of the field into four equal sections. One of these lines, the center line, divides the field in half.

Field hockey—a game of constant movement.

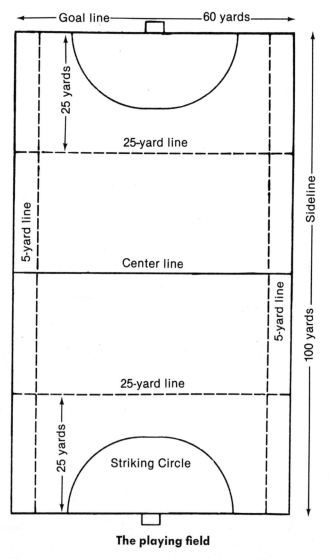

The playing field

On each side of the field, an alley is formed by lines that are five yards inside the sidelines and that run parallel to them.

There are eleven players on each team. Teams are made up of forwards, midfielders, backs, and a goalkeeper.

The goal cages are placed in the center of the goal lines (also called end lines or back lines). The goalposts are 7 feet (2.1 meters) high and 12 feet or 4 yards (3.7 meters) apart. They are connected by a crossbar. A net is attached to the posts and the crossbar.

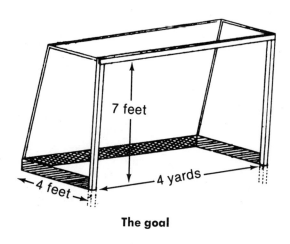

The goal

Each player carries a stick with a curved end which is flat on the left side and rounded on the right side. Only the flat side may be used to hit the ball. Sticks are from 34 to 37 inches in length.

The ball, from $8\frac{13}{16}$ to $9\frac{1}{4}$ inches in circumference, about the size of a softball, has a cork and twine center and a leather cover. It weighs from $5\frac{1}{2}$ to $5\frac{3}{4}$ ounces.

In high school play, a game lasts 50 minutes. It is divided into two 25-minute halves with a 10-minute rest period between them. At halftime, teams change ends.

Players try to advance the ball with their sticks until they are in a position to shoot at the other team's goal. Scoring a goal counts one point. Scores of typical games are 2-1 or 3-2.

A goal can only occur when a player hits the ball over the goal line and into the goal cage from the nearly semicircular area in front of each goal called the striking circle or shooting circle. Each striking circle is composed of two quarter circles, each with a radius of 16 yards (13.7 meters) drawn from the goal with each goal post as a center. The circles are joined by a line that is 4 yards (3.7 meters) in length and that is parallel to the goal line.

The game starts with a bully. Two opposing players at the center of the field stand over the ball, facing one another and the opposite sideline. Each strikes her stick on the ground beside the ball and strikes her opponent's stick just above the ball. This action is repeated three times. Then each player tries to gain possession of the ball or pass to a teammate. There is a bully after each goal.

No body contact or dangerous hitting is permitted. Fouls are called whenever a player:

• Raises any part of her stick above the level of her shoulder when playing or attempting to play the ball, a violation called "sticks."

• Plays the ball with the rounded side of her stick.

• Trips, shoves, pushes, charges, strikes at, or in any way contacts an opponent.

• Strikes, hits, hooks, holds, or in any way interferes with an opponent's stick.

• Undercuts the ball or hits in any way that causes the ball to rise dangerously.

• Stops the ball with any part of her body other than her hand. If the ball is caught, it must be dropped immediately; it cannot be thrown or carried.

• Kicks the ball. Stopping the ball with one's foot counts as kicking. (An exception is made in the case of the goalie. Provided she is within the striking circle, the goalkeeper is permitted to stop the ball with her feet, kick it, and allow it to rebound off of any part of her body.)

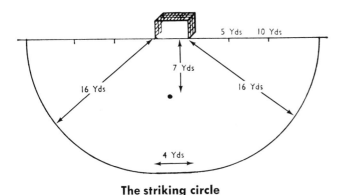

5 Yds   10 Yds

7 Yds

16 Yds   16 Yds

4 Yds

The striking circle

- Hits or passes the ball between her feet.
- Runs between an opponent and the ball.
- Participates in the game without a stick.

Two umpires control the game, with each responsible for one half of the playing field area. However, each official watches activity on the entire sideline area on her side of the field.

Fouls that occur outside the striking circle are penalized by awarding a free hit to the offended team. When a free hit is called, all players must stay at least five yards from the ball. A member of the offended team then hits the ball from the point where the violation occurred.

If the attacking team commits a foul within the striking circle, the defending team is awarded a free hit from anywhere within the circle.

Violations of the rules can also be penalized by the long corner or short corner. The long corner is a free hit awarded a member of the attacking team when a member of the defensive team unintentionally drives the ball beyond her own goal line. It's taken from a spot on the sideline or goal line five yards from the corner of the field nearest to where the ball crossed the goal line.

The short corner is a free hit that is awarded a member of the attacking team when a defensive player commits a foul inside the striking circle. In executing a short corner, the ball is placed on the goal line at a point at least ten yards from one of the goal posts, on whichever side of the goal the attacking team prefers.

Umpires control play.

The most flagrant rule violations are penalized with a penalty stroke. This is awarded when a member of the defending team commits a foul, which, in the judgment of the umpire, prevented a goal from being scored. It also serves as punishment when a member of the defending team persistently fouls any member of the attacking team.

The player awarded the penalty shot is permitted to take a shot at the goal from a point only seven yards from the goal line, with only the goalkeeper defending.

The umpires also rule in out-of-bounds situations. After the ball has gone out of bounds across a sideline, the umpire decides which team last touched the ball; she then awards the ball to the other team.

The ball is put back in play by means of a push-in, a shot executed by means of a flat, hard stroke that causes the ball to travel along the ground.

When the attacking team causes the ball to go out of bounds over the goal line, the defensive team is awarded a 16-yard hit out. The ball is placed down 16 yards from the goal line and at a point opposite where it crossed the line. A member of the defensive team then hits it.

There are also rules to cover offside situations. These rules are necessary to prevent members of the offensive team from staying close to the goal they're attacking for long periods of time.

According to the rules, a player is offside if she is ahead of a teammate who shoots for the goal unless:

- The player is in her own half of the field.
- There are at least two opponents between her and the goal.

When a team is guilty of an offside violation, the opposing team is awarded a free hit.

For a complete rundown of the rules, obtain a copy of the official rule book. It's available at no charge from the U.S. Field Hockey Association (4415 Buffalo Road, North Chili, NY 14514).

TACTICS

In recent years, field hockey strategies have developed several different offensive systems. These are meant to open up the field, creating more passing and scoring opportunities.

Field hockey's traditional playing system was the 5-3-2. This consisted of five forwards, three halfbacks, and two fullbacks. There was also a player who guarded the goal, of course.

During the 1970s, the 5-3-2 began to give way to the 4-2-3-1 and the 3-3-3-1. The 4-2-3-1 is made up of an attacking line of four forwards. There are two midfield players, called links, three backs, and a sweeper (and the goalie). The key players in the 4-2-3-1 are the links and the sweeper. The links can combine with the four members of the forward line in attacking, or they can drop back to join with the backs in turning aside an opposition thrust.

In the 3-3-3-1, there are three forwards, three links, three backs, and a sweeper (plus the goalie). As in the 4-2-3-1, the links and the sweeper have key roles to play.

Not the 4-2-3-1, the 3-3-3-1, nor any other formation makes for a winning team in itself. Success depends on how well players execute their assignments, not how they happen to be arranged on the field.

No matter what formation your team uses, there are certain tactics you should employ whenever your

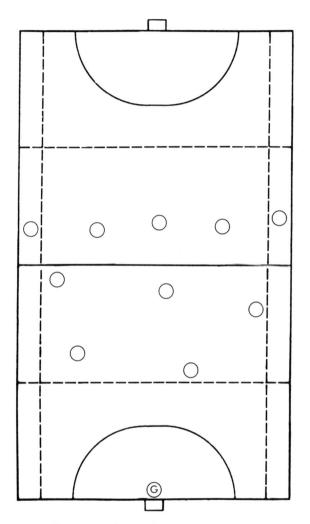

The 5-3-2, the traditional formation

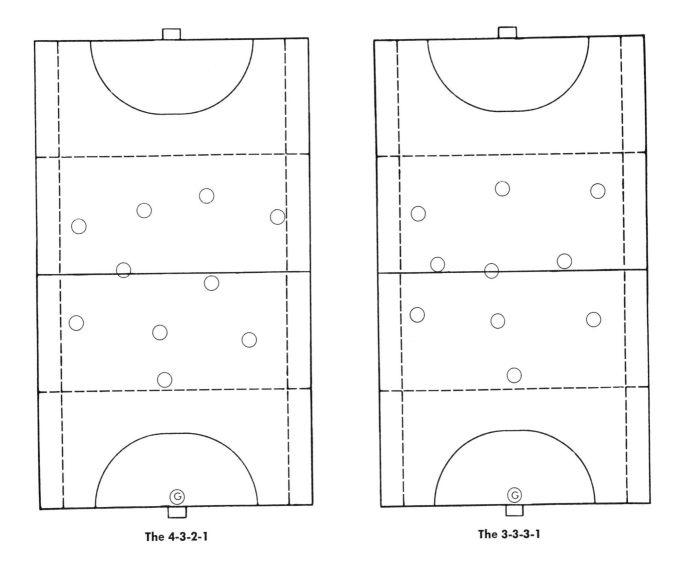

The 4-3-2-1   The 3-3-3-1

On the attack. More and more, success in field hockey depends on movement, on drawing enemy players away from the ball, on "creating space" for your teammates.

team is on the attack. These are basic to your team's success. Be quick to help any teammate who has possession of the ball. Do all you can to draw defensive players away from her. Work to create space through which your teammate can pass or dribble.

Slant into any area in which you can receive a pass.

More and more, field hockey is becoming a game of movement. When you're in motion, you cause problems for the defense while at the same time create options for your teammate with the ball.

THE PLAYING POSITIONS

Field hockey is a game of specialists. Each forward line is made up of attacking players, experts in passing and shooting. Midfielders, or links, support the forward line when the opposition goal is under attack, keeping alert for scoring opportunities. They also play an important defensive role when the opposition has the ball. Defensive players—known as backs—guard, or mark, the opposing forwards closely. The sweeper supports the backs. The goalkeeper is her team's last line of defense.

No matter what your primary assignment happens to be, you have to be able to change responsibilities as the ball changes possession. Soccer and basketball are other sports in which such versatility is expected. If you're a forward, for example, and the other team takes over the ball, you have to immediately assume a defensive role, working to tackle or intercept a pass in your efforts to get the ball back.

The forward line can be made up of as many as five players. There's the center forward who plays in a lane between the two sidelines. There are two wings, forwards who play on the outside of the attacking line. And there are two inners, forwards who are stationed between the center forward and the wings.

You have to be able to run fast to be a forward. Speed is essential in order to be able to get free to receive a pass, or, when you're in possession of the ball, to outrace the defender.

Forwards are the team's best passers and shooters.

Quickness and agility are important, too. You have to be able to make quick starts and to swerve and stop abruptly. When the ball is lost, you have to be able to reverse your field instantly to pursue the opponent with the ball.

The whole idea of the forward line is for the members to work together to get the ball into the opponent's cage. This means you have to be skilled in controlling the ball and be able to pass accurately over long distances. When the ball arrives, it should be at your teammate's stick, not several feet ahead of her.

The center forward directs the team's offense, often deciding which side of the field will be used in attacking. It's her long passes to the wings that frequently trigger her team's scoring charge. She

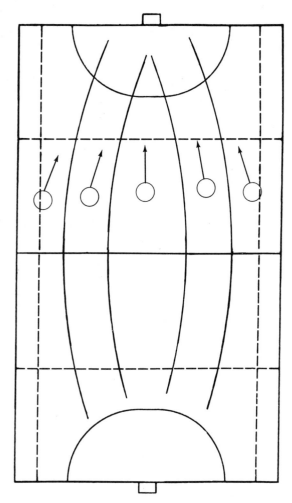

Areas of the field covered by members of the forward line.

warns any member of the forward line who happens to get out of position. It takes leadership qualities to play this position. Since the center forward usually gets more chances to shoot and pass than any other player on the team, she has to be exceptionally skilled in all of the game's strokes and moves.

If you play one of the wing positions, you should always be looking for an opportunity to set up a teammate with a scoring pass or trying to score yourself. Keep within the alley area of the field, if possible. This strings out the defense, giving your team a greater opportunity to score. The wings are usually the best dribblers on the team.

Inners are often the team's playmakers. They each must be able to dribble skillfully and be deft in passing, with their passes usually going to the wings. They're also expected to be good tacklers; in fact, they're usually the best tacklers in the forward line. In the striking area, it's the inners who are assigned to rush in and follow up shots on the goal.

When a team is on the attack, the forward line does not move in a straight line like a string of paraders. An inner might dart several yards ahead of her teammates in the line, penetrating the opposition defense, looking for a pass. If she's tightly marked, she drops back, and the other inner shoots ahead. There's constant forward-and-back movement as the forwards advance.

Sometimes the inners switch positions as an attack is getting underway. The right inner darts over to

Backs must be aggressive tacklers.

play the left side of the field, and the left inner switches to the right side, a move meant to confuse the defense.

On some teams, one or two of the forwards will be designated midfielders or links. Theirs is a key role. They serve as playmakers on offense. Often they're the best play passers on the team. They're also expected to be sure tacklers.

The backs, as defensive specialists, must be aggressive players, experts in tackling. Stamina is a quality that backs require. There's little time to rest or relax. You have to be able to tackle hard, field the ball surely, clear the ball, intercept passes, de-

fend the goal when the offense knifes through, and back up the forwards when your team takes over the attack.

The right and left back usually guard, or mark, the opposing wings. You can't free-lance if you're a back; instead, you must work closely with the back on the opposite side of the field. When the opposition has the ball on the left side of the field, say, the left back dashes forward, and the right back drops back. The center back remains in between her two teammates, and a diagonal line is thus created.

The center back plays the same role on defense as the center forward does on offense, overseeing the

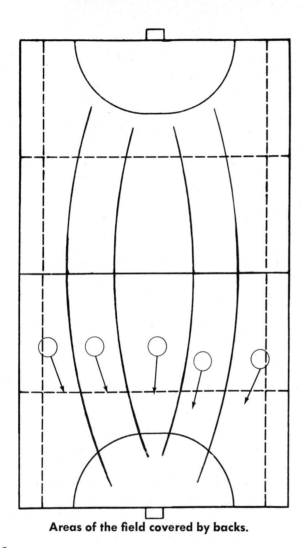

Areas of the field covered by backs.

play of the other backs and cautioning them when they're playing too deep or not deep enough. Often her specific assignment is to cover the center forward, seeking to intercept passes that are directed to her or moving in to make the tackle should she get the ball.

On some teams, deep backs are designated fullbacks. They seldom go beyond the field's center line. In other words, there's not as much running involved in this position. But fullbacks have to be sure tacklers. Like the other backs, the fullbacks must work together as a team. When one advances, the other drops back.

Much of what's said above applies to the sweeper. She supports the backs, keeping alert to intercept a ball that gets through the defense or to tackle an attacker who breaks into the clear. Speed and aggressiveness are what's needed for this position. Often the sweeper directs her team's defense.

The goalkeeper has to stay alert every minute she is on the field, even when her team is on the attack. She can never take her eyes from the ball. The goalkeeper's duties are covered in detail in another section of this book.

It's not only vital that you know the responsibilities that go with your position, but you should also know what your teammates are supposed to be doing as play moves up and down the field. Without that knowledge, you can't expect to be an effective player, either offensively or defensively.

EQUIPMENT

Playing field hockey well begins with getting a stick that "feels" right in your hands and enables you to hit the ball with authority and precision.

Sticks vary in weight from 16 to 21 ounces, and in length from 34 to 37 inches. The weight of the stick may be imprinted on the handle in ounces, or it may be referred to as VL (very light, 16 or 17 ounces); L (light, 18 ounces); M (medium, 19 to 20 ounces); or H (heavy, 21 ounces and over).

How the weight is distributed is important, too. It should be concentrated at the blade end, the hitting end, yet the stick should have a balanced feeling when you swing it.

You also must choose a stick that's the right length. Try this test: Stand erect and place the bottom of the stick blade on the ground beside you. Hold the stick upright. The top of the stick, if it's the right size for you, should come within three or four inches of the hip bone.

Take your time choosing a stick. Too short a stick will cause you to top the ball or miss it completely when you swing. With a stick that's too long, you're likely to hit the ground behind the ball.

During the fury of play, your legs can be accidentally struck with a stick or the ball. Protect your legs with shin guards. Light in weight, they fit inside the heavy socks field hockey players wear.

Your mouth and teeth need protection, too. Don't

Stick length test: With the blade on the ground, handle end should come within about three or four inches of your hip bone.

Shin guards protect the legs.

23

Shoes for field hockey have cleated heels and soles.

take part in a game or practice session without wearing a plastic mouthguard, the same type worn by ice hockey and football players.

Field hockey shoes have cleated soles and heels. They should fit snugly but be comfortable, too. Lightness and flexibility are other qualities to look for.

For uniforms, short pleated skirts—kilts—are popular, particularly in the Northeast. Tunics are worn as uniforms, too, usually by junior high or prep school players. Wraparound skirts are winning acceptance, and some teams, chiefly in the West, prefer shorts.

Shirts can be short or long-sleeved. Raglan sleeves permit the freedom of arm movement you need.

What's said above applies to all players, except the goalkeeper. The specialized equipment the goalkeeper wears is discussed later in this book.

Pleated skirts—kilts—are traditional uniform for field hockey.

THE STROKES

Whenever you pass to a teammate, shoot, or clear the ball, you use one of several basic strokes. Try to become accomplished in executing them all. Practice with a partner who is 30 or 40 feet away from you, hitting the ball back and forth.

If you're a beginner, learn to grip the stick with this drill: Lay the stick on the ground so that it extends outward from where you're standing, the handle end at your feet. The blade should point to the left.

Reach down with your left hand and grasp the stick near the end of the handle. Simply "shake hands" with the handle.

Picking the stick up by the handle, swing the

To get proper grip, pick up stick from ground as shown, gripping handle with your left hand. Swing the stick blade to the right, and then grasp handle with your right hand.

Left hand is always positioned at handle end; right hand, below.

blade toward your right side, grasping the stick with your right hand. Notice how the blade is now in an ideal position for hitting the ball.

The left hand should always be positioned near the handle end. The right hand grips below it. How far below depends on the type of stroke you're executing. If you're driving the ball, the right hand

should be close to the left, just touching it. If the stroke is to be a flick, the right hand should be at about the center of the stick.

THE DRIVE—The drive is a versatile stroke, used for passing, shooting, and clearing. As the game's most powerful stroke, it's possible to achieve extremely long distances with it. Some advanced players can drive the ball all the way from one end of the field to the other.

When you want to drive the ball, your hands should be together on the handle, and you swing the stick in pendulumlike fashion, the blade facing in the direction you want the ball to travel. In your enthusiasm to hit hard, don't allow the stick to go higher than shoulder level on either the backswing or forward swing. If this happens, it's a foul—called "sticks"—and a penalty will be assessed against your team.

To execute a drive, step toward the ball with your left foot as you lift the stick into the backswing. At the top of the backswing, your wrists should be cocked, and your weight concentrated on your right foot.

With your eyes fixed on the ball, swing the stick forward, shifting your weight to the left side. Keep your wrists and forearms firm. Make contact with the ball at the center of the blade.

Follow through, the stick moving in the direction the ball is traveling. But, remember, don't permit the stick to swing any higher than shoulder level.

Topping the ball is a common problem in attempt-

When you drive, get your body into the swing. Your weight should be concentrated on your right side as you draw the stick into the backswing. Then shift your weight to the left side as you swing the stick through.

ing to drive. The blade strikes the upper half of the ball and it travels only a few feet as a result. Topping is usually caused by taking your eyes off the ball, maybe glancing up for a split second to look for your receiver. Learn to glue your eyes on the ball from the start of the stroke until the follow-through begins.

THE FLICK—Coaches agree that this is field hockey's most important stroke. Not only is it a fairly powerful stroke, but it enables you to be accurate, to put the ball right on target.

In executing a flick, you lift the ball off the

With a quick wrist snap and the shifting of the weight to the left side, the ball is flicked into the air.

There's no backswing in the flick. It begins from this position, the right knee deeply bent.

ground and it travels a good part of the way in the air. Forwards use the flick in shooting because it's a difficult shot for the goalie to handle. It's a good stroke to use when passing or when seeking to elude an opponent who is blocking your path.

Your hands should be well apart on the stick when you flick the ball, the right hand at about the stick's midpoint. Play the ball farther forward than when you drive. It should be positioned about in front of your left foot.

There's no backswing in the flick. Simply place the stick blade behind the ball. Bend from the waist. Bend in the knees.

Get the lower edge of the blade under the ball. Then whip the ball into the air with a quick movement of your wrists and by shifting your weight from your right to left side. Imagine that the stick blade is "throwing" the ball, almost as if the stick is an extension of your arm.

THE PUSH—The push is a stroke that is sometimes described as being halfway between a drive and a flick. It is a gentle stroke, usually used when you want to get the ball to a teammate who is only a short distance away.

The hands should be six or seven inches apart. There's no backswing. Again, simply place the stick blade behind the ball.

Once the stick is in position, the right hand and arm sweep the blade along the ground, "pushing" the ball toward its target. At the same time, you shift your weight from the right to left side. As the

In the push stroke, begin by placing the blade behind the ball. Right wrist and hand push the ball toward the target as the body's weight shifts to the left.

stroke is completed, your stick and arms should be extended in the direction the ball is to travel.

THE SCOOP—When you execute the scoop, another gentle stroke, you shovel the ball up into the air. It travels only a short distance. While it can be useful when you're in tight quarters, you don't see the scoop very often. You can go an entire game, even several games, without using it.

Like the flick, the scoop is a wristy shot. You must get the stick blade under the ball as you shoot, "scooping" the ball into the air with a shoveling motion.

The time you spend getting the blade in position under the ball can give an opponent time to tackle you or, at the very least, get into position defensively. That's why the scoop isn't used very often.

Stroking the ball successfully requires more than merely physical skill. Whenever you execute a drive or flick, a push or scoop, you should have a target in mind. Some beginners simply whack the ball aimlessly upfield whenever they gain possession, hoping there will be a teammate around when the ball arrives.

An experienced player maps out strategy, perhaps executing a dodge or dribbling before passing or shooting. When she does stroke the ball, she never fails to target on a teammate's stick or the goal.

For a scoop shot, you must first get the blade under the ball. Use a shoveling stroke.

To drive the ball to the right, use reverse stick, revolving the handle in your hands one half turn. That puts the flat side of the blade behind the ball, permitting you to drive the ball away.

REVERSE STICK

The previous section explains hitting the ball in the manner you're going to be hitting it most of the time, to the left.

But suppose you want to hit in the opposite direction, from left to right. The rules prohibit you from hitting with the rounded side of the stick. To get the flat side of the blade behind the ball, you have to position yourself on the other side, changing your position by 180 degrees.

A simpler and quicker method is to use reverse stick. As you grip the stick, spin the handle one half turn. Now the tip of the blade is pointing toward the ground and the flat side of the blade is behind the ball. You can now drive the ball to the right.

DRIBBLING

Dribbling is the term used to describe the way you advance the ball, hitting it with a series of light taps with the flat side of your stick blade.

Keep the ball to your right as you dribble. Your hands should be several inches apart on the stick.

As you run, keep the ball ahead of your lead foot and a bit to the outside of your right foot. This enables you to run freely and lessens the possibility of your kicking the ball.

How hard you hit depends to some degree on where the opposition players are positioned. If an opponent happens to be closing in on you, you'll want to keep the ball close to your stick, merely tapping it lightly. If no opposition players are close by, you can hit the ball sharply. But keep it under control, of course.

Keep your eyes on the ball as you dribble, but occasionally glance around to get an idea of what your teammates and the defensive players are doing.

As you become skilled in dribbling, learn to vary your pace. A slow dribble gives your teammates time to get free. Dribbling fast can help you avoid being tackled.

In dribbling, advancing the ball as you run, tap the ball lightly, keeping it off to your right side and in front of your lead foot.

A common dodge involves hitting the ball to your left, past the onrushing opponent on her stick side, and then swerving in that direction to retrieve it.

DODGING

When you're racing toward your opponent's goal with the ball, and an enemy player moves to tackle you, you can either pass or dodge. Passing is whacking the ball to a teammate. Dodging is keeping the ball yourself while eluding the tackler.

Anytime you attempt a dodge, you should have the ball under full control. Proper footwork is also vital. Be sure to get your feet and body moving in the direction you plan to go before you strike the ball; otherwise, you won't be successful.

There are several types of dodges. The most common is the pull to the left, used when an opponent is rushing up head-on to tackle you. As the player approaches, suddenly swerve to the left, then rap

You can also dodge by hitting the ball to your right, past your opponent on her nonstick side. Then cut in the opposite direction, circling around her, to recover the ball.

the ball in that direction. Once you regain possession, take off in the direction of the goal. You can use this dodge anywhere on the field.

Another common dodge involves driving the ball past your opponent on her left side, her nonstick side, as she moves to tackle. Then dart around her on the other side, recovering the ball.

Try to keep calm when a tackler rushes toward you. Planning in advance what dodge you're going to use will help to give you more confidence.

Passes have to be properly timed, so the receiver can take the ball on the run.

PASSING

Good passing is as vital to field hockey success as sticks and cleated shoes. Forwards pass to one another to elude defensive players and advance the ball toward the opposition goal. Defenders pass to the forwards to get the ball to them as fast and as safely as possible. There's no faster, surer method of moving the ball.

The drive and the flick are the strokes usually used in passing. Push passes can be effective when the ball is to cover only a short distance.

You must never be haphazard about your passes. Each has to be accurate; each has to be properly

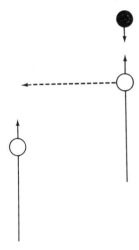

Square pass (broken line), with the passer aiming ahead of the receiver, so she can take the ball without breaking stride.

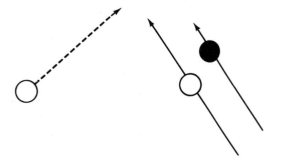

Diagonal pass, with the receiver cutting in front of defensive player.

timed. The pass should be placed so that your teammate can receive the ball on the run, without having to slow down.

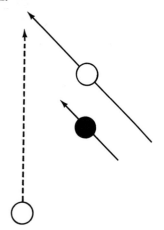

Through pass, the ball hit in a direction parallel to the sideline.

What's said above means that you must know your target in advance. This applies whether you're passing to a teammate or to an open area between teammates. It takes planning to be a good passer.

As the diagrams in this section indicate, passes can be directed to one side or the other, diagonally, or forward or back.

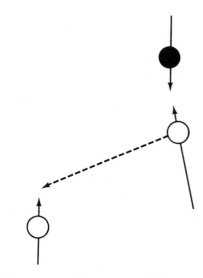

Back pass, used here to avoid being tackled.

RECEIVING PASSES

When receiving the ball from a teammate, keep your hands well apart on the stick and let the blade "give" a little to absorb the ball's impact.

Always give your teammate a target, indicating with the blade where you want the ball to go. You should be able to take the ball on the run without breaking stride.

It's important to glue your eyes to the ball as it approaches. Keep watching it until it makes contact with the blade.

If you're a beginner, learning to control the ball as it comes bounding along the ground toward you can be difficult. The problem may be that the ball rebounds off the blade, and you end up chasing it.

The solution probably rests with your wrists. Keep your wrists relaxed as the ball approaches, and allow them to "give" slightly as the ball makes contact with the blade. In that way, the blade will "give," too, and there won't be any rebound.

What's said above refers to passes that come toward you from your left side. Since these arrive at the flat side of the blade, they're the easiest to handle.

Passes from the right side are more difficult. Step across the path of the oncoming ball with your left foot. At the same time, swing your stick to the right side of your body, facing the flat-blade surface toward the ball.

In receiving a pass, allow the stick to "give" as the ball makes contact.

If the ball is a good distance out in front of you and there's no chance to step across its path, you'll have to receive the ball with the stick reversed. Keep your hands well apart on the handle and turn the tip of the blade of the stick toward the ground.

Once you have the ball under control, you're ready for your next move—dribbling, passing, or shooting.

SHOOTING

Any legal stroke—the drive, flick, push, or scoop—can be used for a shot on goal. Whatever shot you use, it must be executed from within the striking circle.

When you're shooting from near the outer edge of the striking circle, it's usually best to drive the ball. In closer, the flick is more effective.

Getting the shot away quickly is vital. As soon as you enter the striking circle, shoot. Carrying the ball too far into the circle gives the defense, including the goalie, time to get into position to block the shot.

Aim for the side of the goal on which the goalie is holding her stick, getting the ball as high as you can. High on her stick side is where the goalie is the most vulnerable. Shots that go to her other side can often be snared with her glove hand. But she can't make gloved saves on her stick side.

The goalie can block shots along the ground with her feet. That's why it's important to get the ball into the air.

Following up the shot is as important as the shot itself. The ball is likely to rebound off the goalkeeper's pads or one of the goalposts. By rushing in, you or one of your teammates may get a second scoring chance before the defense clears the ball.

Goalie is most vulnerable high on her stick side (circled area).

Center back clears from a point not far from the midfield line.

CLEARING

Clearing is a defensive move in which you drive the ball away from the goal you're defending, targeting on a teammate, often a wing, or at least on an open area that you expect a teammate to occupy. Every player has to know how to clear.

It's always important to clear the ball, not merely away from your goal, but, generally speaking, toward the nearest sideline. If you send the ball toward the center of the field, an interception is likely to result. That's because the middle of the field is usually clogged with players.

If play is within the striking circle in front of the

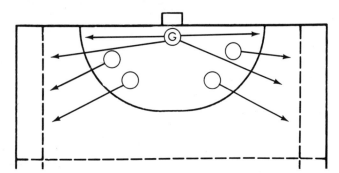

Typical clearing shots from within the shooting circle.

goal you're defending and you recover the ball, you'll be so tightly covered you won't be able to pass, only dribble and dodge. But as soon as you're in the clear, pass to a wing near the closest sideline.

When play is between the striking circle and the 25-yard line and you gain possession of the ball, you're likely to have more passing options. A halfback can angle the ball upfield to a forward; a fullback can target on a halfback.

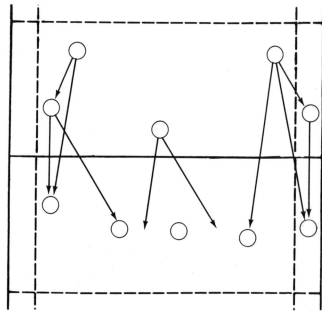

Clearing shots when close to the center line.

THE BULLY

The bully is a method of putting the ball in play at the beginning of the game, after halftime, or following the scoring of a goal. Although similar to the face-off in ice hockey or lacrosse, the bully is one of field hockey's most distinctive features.

To conduct a bully, two opposing players stand over the ball facing each other and the opposite sidelines. They strike their sticks on the ground beside the ball and then strike them together over the ball. They then repeat this sequence two more times, and then each quickly attempts to gain possession of the ball or pass to a teammate.

All this action unfolds in a matter of seconds, which means the action is somewhat frantic. You have to be quick and determined to win a bully.

If you're assigned to take part in a bully, stand with your feet comfortably apart, your weight on the balls of your feet. Your hands should be well apart as you grip the stick. Bend deeply from the waist as you get set. You should be looking almost straight down at the ball.

Don't worry about what your opponent is going to try to do. Instead, you set the pace. This is especially true on the third and final touching of your sticks. At this point, speed up your stick work so that you get to the ball first.

Know in advance which one of several methods you're going to use in gaining control of the ball.

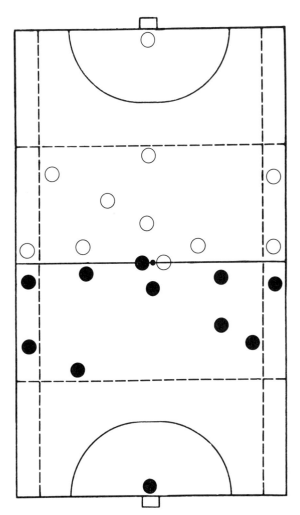

Position of players for a bully.

Bully action is always fast and furious. You have to
be quick and determined to end up with the ball.

A standard method is to simply trap the ball with the stick blade and deftly draw it toward you, back-pedaling as you do. Pass to a teammate before your opponent reacts.

Another tactic involves reverse stick. After hitting your opponent's stick for the third time, give the stick handle a half turn in your hands, reversing the position of the blade, and then rap the ball back to a teammate.

Still another method is to step toward the ball and poke it through your opponent's legs. Then swerve around her to take possession. Don't be so eager to hit the ball that you swat it to an opposition player. This happens quite frequently.

Sometimes both participants in the bully seek to hit the ball in the same way, and the ball gets wedged in between their sticks as a result. Should this happen, keep pressing the ball hard against your opponent's stick, and then suddenly raise your blade slightly. The ball will jump over her stick blade. Then it's up to you to pounce on it.

When a bully is underway, each team lines up within the half of the field it's defending. All players, except the two taking part in the bully, must keep at least five yards from the ball. If you're not actually participating in the bully, you must still keep alert, ready to receive a pass or tackle an opponent. It's a critical moment, for you don't know until the action is completed whether your team is going to be attacking or defending.

TACKLING

When an opposing player has the ball at her stick, you're not permitted to hit, shove, or trip her in seeking to gain control of the ball. All you're allowed to do is tackle her.

But tackling in field hockey is not like the tackling you've seen in football. The term means simply knocking the ball away from the ball handler's control in an effort to gain possession yourself. Tackling goes on constantly in every field hockey game.

You must always tackle cleanly, of course. You don't want to get penalized for obstructing with your shoulder or stick.

Keep your eyes on the ball when you move to tackle. Grip the stick firmly in both hands. As you approach your opponent, bend from the waist, keeping the stick blade on the ground, ready to steal the ball away at the first opportunity.

Once you have the ball in your possession, dribble away fast or pass to a teammate. Don't give your opponent the chance to tackle *you*.

In approaching an opponent head-on, get your stick to the ground in front of the ball. Try to figure out in which direction she plans to go. Then move accordingly. Use some deception—a hip, head, or shoulder fake—in an effort to get her to move in a particular direction.

Jab at the ball or at your opponent's stick. This can cause her to give up the ball or make her pass hurriedly.

44

In making a head-on tackle, hold your stick low to

When chasing an opponent who is dribbling the ball, get even with her before you attempt to tackle. Overtake her on the right side. Now the two of you are running side-by-side. Holding your stick in your

the ground as you approach. When you get close, jab at the ball or your opponent's stick.

left hand, swing the blade at the ball, knocking it free.

Coming up on the other side, the left side, is more difficult. Once you overtake the ball carrier, circle around in front of her. As you circle, get your stick on the ball and pull it with you. If you're successful, you'll end up on your opponent's right side and with the ball on your blade.

45

When pursuing an opponent with the ball, get side-by-side with her, and then try to knock the ball free.

THE PUSH-IN

After the ball has gone out of bounds across a sideline, it is put back in play by means of a push-in. The umpire decides which team last touched the ball, then awards the push-in to the other team.

You have to use a push shot when executing a push-in, and the ball must travel along the ground. If the ball goes above knee level, possession is given over to the other team. The player taking the shot

Push-in is a method of putting the ball in play after it's gone over a sideline.

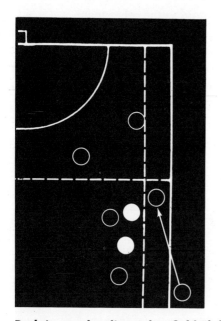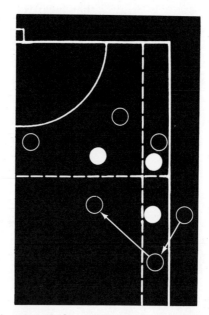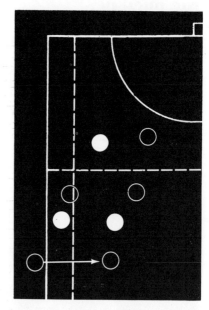

Push-in can be directed upfield (*left*), toward the goal you're attacking. Back pass (*center*), is another push-in alternative, with receiver passing goalward. You can send the push-in toward the center of the field, too (*right*).

cannot play the ball a second time until it has been touched by another player.

All players, both offensive and defensive, must be at least five yards away from the ball as the shot is executed. All sticks must be flat to the ground. Basketball's throw-in is similar to field hockey's push-in.

If you're assigned to execute a push-in, turn to face the goal your team is attacking. If you're fairly close to your own goal, try pushing the ball to a back. But if the ball is placed down close to the goal your team has under attack, try to get the pass to a forward in the striking circle, or at least to a teammate who can, in turn, pass to someone there.

MARKING AND COVERING

Marking and covering are field hockey's basic defensive skills.

In marking, you're assigned to guard a particular opponent. The right back often marks the opposition left wing; the right inner, the opposing center forward; and so on.

When you're marking, stay as close to your opponent as you can without obstructing her. "You're right on her stick" is the way one coach puts it.

Keep yourself positioned between your opponent and the ball, so you're in a position to intercept any pass sent to her. Your stick should be low to the ground, only a few inches from her stick.

When should you mark an opponent? It depends

As play surges downfield, covering player at left will move to tackle.

on the position you play and where the ball happens to be. A back, for instance, moves up to mark a forward when the forward gets possession of the ball or when a pass to the forward seems likely.

Marking is vital, of course, when the ball is being played in the striking circle in front of the goal you're defending. In such a situation, you must mark your opponent as tightly as possible, seeking to prevent her from getting a shot at the goal.

If she does happen to get the ball, rush toward her before she can get it under control and shoot. By being aggressive, you may be able to force her to make an error. As you dash in, however, be careful not to block your goalie's view of the play.

Forwards always must mark on free hits and push-ins. On corner hits, players must rush out quickly to mark their assigned players.

When play moves away from the striking circle into the area between the 25-yard line and the center line, you don't have to mark your opponent quite so closely. Keep within two or three yards of her, positioning yourself between her and the goal you're defending. If your opponent should gain possession, make a fast tackle.

Covering is different from marking in that you're defending a particular area of the field, not an opposition player. When you're covering, you might get a chance to intercept a long pass or you may pick up an unmarked opponent who gets through your teammates.

Players who are covering must work together closely. Suppose you're the left back and the ball is passed to the other side of the field, the right side. The right back moves up to cover immediately. At the same time, you should drift back in the direction of the goal you're defending. If the attacker with the ball should get by the right back, you'll be in a position to pick her up. Fullbacks work together in the same fashion; when one moves up to cover, the other drops back.

The basic idea of covering and marking is to gain possession of the ball. If you're the one who gains possession, you should know exactly what you're going to do with it. This means you must keep aware of where your teammates are positioned so that you can pass to one of them.

GOALKEEPING

As the last line of defense, the goalkeeper plays a critical role. What she does is vital not only to the defense, but to the offense as well, for her hard, well-placed clearing shots and kicks are frequently what gets a team's attack underway.

The goalie is permitted to use any part of her body in stopping shots. Thus, she wears special equipment, including a helmet and facemask, thickly cushioned leg pads, and thick pads, called kickers, that cover her shoes. She also wears gloves to take the sting out of catches she makes.

Agility is a must if you're thinking of becoming a goalie. In protecting the mouth of the goal, which is 12 feet wide and 7 feet high, you have to be able to dart fast to your right or left, lashing out at the ball with one of your padded legs. You have to be able to concentrate, keeping your attention focused on the ball, even when it's being played at the opposite end of the field.

The position also takes courage. You have to be able to face an onrushing attacker without flinching and coolly turn aside her attempt to put the ball behind you. And when the ball is driven at your body from only a few yards away, you have to stand up to it, letting it slam into your padded legs or plucking it out of the air with one hand or the other.

Positioning yourself a few feet in front of the goal line, you, as the goalie, should learn to operate out

51

Goalies require the protection offered by a helmet and facemask.

Kickers for the feet and leg pads are also necessary.

Goalies operate out of this basic stance, crouching slightly, leg pads together.

of a basic stance, crouching slightly, your feet together, so your leg pads form one big, rectangular shield. Hold the stick in one hand, gripping it several inches from the end.

As play moves back and forth in front of the goal cage, you should move, too, always keeping your body positioned between the goal line and the ball. When play surges to the right, you adjust to the right.

At times during a game, an attacker will break into the clear and streak for the goal. When this happens, rush toward the attacker and tackle. The sooner you can meet her, the better. You might even be able to make the tackle as she enters the striking circle. Kick the ball away with your instep.

If there's no chance to tackle the lone attacker, move two or three yards out of the goal toward her as she's preparing to shoot. This strategy enables you to reduce the amount of target area she has. It's called "playing the angles." Try this test: Hold one hand a couple of inches from your eyes. All you can see is your fingers and part of the palm. Now extend your arm to its full length, holding your hand as far away from your face as you can. Now you can see the entire hand and part of your arm, and there's plenty of surrounding space.

The same principle applies when you, as a goalie, play the angles. When you move out of the goal and toward the advancing ball carrier, you reduce the amount of space she has as a target. When you re-

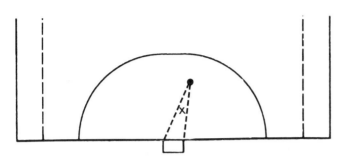

By moving out of the goal (to point x), goalie reduces shooter's target area.

main at the goal line, the attacker's target area swells in size.

While there are several ways to cope with shots, the safest thing to do is use your legs and feet. Let's suppose an attacking player has driven the ball right at you, and it's traveling several inches off the ground. Face the shot squarely, your legs together so your pads are touching. Bend in the knees. As the ball strikes your pads, bend your knees more. This deflects the ball downward near your feet. Clear the ball with a quick kick to the right or left, targeting on your wings. You can also use your stick in clearing, but usually the stick is reserved for emergency situations.

Your object is to get the ball as far away from the goal as you can. To unleash a powerful kick, take a step toward the ball with your nonkicking foot, placing that foot alongside the ball, and then swing the inside of the other foot into the ball.

Shots that arrive head high should be gloved with one hand or the other.

Handle any ball that comes bouncing toward you by getting in front of it and blocking it with your pads. Be sure you have your legs tightly together.

When the ball comes toward you at or above the level of your head, reach up with one hand and catch it. Then immediately drop it to the ground and clear it with a quick kick.

Shots along the ground should be handled with kick saves.

On shots that are wide to the right or left, you'll have to lunge for the ball, thrusting one foot out, making the save with the inside of that foot.

Use your stick to make saves on shots that are far to your right, beyond the range of your right foot. Move with catlike quickness, bending low at the last instant, reaching out with the blade, getting it almost flat to the ground. Stick saves are rare, however. It's safer to use your feet or leg pads.

The penalty stroke presents the goalkeeper with special problems. The member of the attacking team assigned to take the stroke is only seven yards away. While she can't drive the ball at you—only push, scoop, or flick it—she has a big advantage. After all, the shooter knows what she is going to do (or should know). You, as the goalie, don't know; you can only guess.

Watch the shooter carefully and try to get some indication as to what she plans. Notice how she places her stick blade down in relation to the ball. Maybe this will tip off whether she plans to send the ball to the right or the left. Check her grip and the way her weight is balanced.

The rules state that you, as the goalkeeper, are not permitted to move your feet until the ball is touched by the attacker. Standing in the very center of the goal, crouch slightly as she prepares to hit, your feet slightly apart, your weight on the balls of your feet. Grasp your stick in both hands and hold it in front of your body, parallel to the ground.

You're now ready to pounce to either the right or left.

Concentrate. Once the attacker has committed herself to her swing, start lunging to where you believe the ball is going to go.

Don't feel badly if you're beaten. In penalty stroke situations, the odds favor the shooter.

As the goalie, you also have a supervisory role to play. Talk to your teammates when there is action in front of the goal, warning them if they're not properly positioned. If a teammate is blocking your view of the ball and the play, yell at her to get out of the way. When you want to pounce on a ball and clear it, and a teammate has the same plan, shout out, "Mine!" She should step back and allow you to make the play.

In the case of a corner, you may want to have a teammate help you out in the goal. While you position yourself near one goalpost, she guards the goal on the other side. This strategy enables you to move out from the goal toward the player receiving the ball, narrowing her shooting angle.

FREE HITS

In basketball, when a foul is committed, the offended team gets a free throw. In field hockey, when one team breaks a rule, the other team gets a free hit.

The free hit takes place at the spot on the field where the violation occurred. All players, both offensive and defensive, must keep at least five yards away from the ball. Outside of that, there's little formality to the play. The player taking the shot simply steps up and hits the ball, passing to a teammate. Only the push shot may be used in free hit situations; the drive, flick, and scoop are not permitted.

If you're assigned to take a free hit, try to get the shot away as quickly as possible. Delaying gives the defensive team time to get in position.

Of course, there may be times when it's not possible to hit quickly. In such cases, wait for the players to get set, and then look for one of your teammates to make a move that will get her free.

If the offensive team fouls within the striking circle, the defensive player taking the shot can execute it from anywhere within the circle. If you're designated to take a free hit in this situation, it's best to execute the shot from the spot where the ball is placed down, rather than try to dribble in and shoot.

The 16-yard hit out is a particular type of free hit. It is awarded to a member of the defending team in each of these situations:

On free hits, all players must keep at least five yards away from ball.

• When a member of the offensive team hits the ball over the back line (but not between the goal-posts).

• When a member of the offensive team hits the ball between the goal posts from any point outside the striking circle.

• When a member of the defensive team unintentionally hits the ball over the goal line from any point beyond the 25-yard line.

In each case, the ball is placed down 16 yards from the goal line at a point opposite where it crossed the goal line. The defensive team player is then permitted an unhindered shot.

If you're assigned to take such a shot, quickly get the ball to the nearest wing. If you're shooting from the right side of the field, pass to the wing on your right. She'll then send the ball upfield. What you must never do is pass the ball in the other direction, so it crosses in front or goes through the striking circle. An interception could easily result, and a shot on goal would almost certainly follow.

CORNERS

Corners are free hits, too, and very important ones. When planned and executed properly, a corner should result in a shot on the goal.

There are two types of corners—the long corner and short corner, also known as the penalty corner.

The long corner is a free shot awarded a member of the attacking team when a defender drives the ball beyond her own goal line. It's taken from a spot on the sidelines or goal line five yards from the corner of the field nearest to where the ball went out of bounds.

The short corner is awarded the attacking team when a foul is committed by a defender inside the striking circle. The ball is placed on the goal line at least ten yards from one of the goalposts, whichever post the attacking team prefers.

Usually it's a wing who takes the corner hit. The other members of the forward line take up positions just within the striking circle. The backs get in position behind the forwards, ready to field the ball should it be missed.

The defending team uses tactics that are unique. Six defensive players, usually the backs and goalie, position themselves behind the goal line. Each of these players is responsible for covering a particular offensive player, and lines up opposite that player.

The wing hits the ball hard to one of her for-

On corner hits, six defensive players line up behind the goal line. As the offensive player hits the ball, the defensive players rush into the field of play, trying to get possession of the ball or to block the ensuing shot.

wards. The forward stops the ball, then slams it toward the goal. (The rules require that the ball be controlled before it can be hit; you can't hit it on the fly.)

But the instant the wing hits the ball to the forward, the defensive players swoop from behind the goal line, seeking to thwart the shot. It's a moment of high excitement.

THE PENALTY STROKE

A penalty stroke, introduced to field hockey in 1974, is awarded when a member of the defending team has committed a flagrant foul or a foul which, in the judgment of the referee, prevents a goal from being scored. It can also be awarded when a member of the defending team persistently fouls any member of the attacking team.

Only the player awarded the shot and the goalkeeper participate. The other players must remain beyond the 25-yard line. The ball is placed down seven yards from the goal.

Several restrictions are placed on the shooter, who is designated by her coach and can be any member of the offended team. She can't belt the ball as hard as she wants to; she can't drive it. Only the push, scoop, and flick are permitted. And in executing any of these, the shooter is not permitted to take more than one stride.

The rules governing the penalty stroke also specify that the goalie may not move her feet until the ball is touched.

Obviously, it's a guessing game, with the odds favoring the shooter. If you're assigned to take a penalty stroke, make up your mind in advance where

In penalty stroke situations, the advantage is with the shooter.

you plan to place the ball. Remember, the goalie is the most vulnerable high on her stick side.

Watch the goalie carefully as she takes her stance. She may commit herself by leaning slightly in the direction she intends to move. If she's leaning to the right, try placing the ball in the goal's upper left-hand corner. But be careful you don't tip off what you plan to do.

GLOSSARY

ALLEY—The area of the playing field between the sideline and a line five yards inside and parallel to the sideline.

BACK—Any one of the three to five primarily defensive players who is positioned closest to the goal line her team is defending. Also called halfback.

BLADE—The striking surface of the stick.

BULLY—A method of putting the ball in play in which two opposing players stand over the ball and face one another, strike their sticks to the ground beside the ball and then together over it three times, and then attempt to gain possession of the ball or pass it to a teammate.

CENTER FORWARD—The forward who plays in the middle of the attacking line, between the two inners.

CLEAR—To drive the ball away from the goal line being defended.

CORNER—A free hit awarded the attacking team for one of several rule violations on the part of the defensive team. *See* Long corner, Short corner.

COVERING—Guarding a particular area of the field.

DODGE—A maneuver in which the player with the ball eludes a defender, while keeping possession of the ball.

DRIBBLE—To advance the ball with a series of light taps.

DRIVE—A hard stroke that travels on a relatively flat trajectory.

FIELD HOCKEY ASSOCIATION OF AMERICA—The governing body of men's field hockey in the United States.

FLICK—A shot made without any backswing that causes the ball to lift into the air.

FORWARD—Any one of the three to five offensive players who plays closest to the goal her team is attacking.

FREE HIT—The unhindered hit of a stationary ball a player is awarded when an opposing player commits a foul.

FULLBACK—A primarily defensive player who is stationed between the goal her team is defending and the other backs.

GOALIE, GOALKEEPER — The defensive player who is stationed in front of the goal she is defending, and whose duty it is to keep the ball from going into the goal.

HALFBACK—*See* Back.

INNER—A forward who is stationed between the center forward and a wing.

INTERNATIONAL FEDERATION OF WOMEN'S FIELD HOCKEY ASSOCIATIONS—The governing body of women's field hockey worldwide.

KICKERS—Pads worn by the goalie to protect the feet.

LINK—A forward who is stationed between the forward line and the backs.

LONG CORNER—A free hit awarded the attacking team when a member of the defensive team unintentionally drives the ball beyond her own goal line.

MARK—To guard an opponent closely.

MIDFIELDER—One of three or four players who are stationed between the forwards and the backs.

OFFSIDE—For a player to be in the attacking half of the field when there are fewer than two defenders nearer the goal at the time a teammate plays the ball. When a team is called for offside, the opposition team is awarded a free hit.

PENALTY CORNER—*See* Short corner.

PENALTY SHOT—An unhindered shot at the goal, which is defended only by the goalkeeper, awarded to a member of the attacking team for a serious infraction of the rules by a member of the defensive team.

PUSH—A shot made without any backswing in which the blade is swept along the ground, "pushing" the ball toward the target.

PUSH-IN—The method of putting the ball in play after it has gone out of bounds over a sideline.

REVERSE STICK—A method of hitting the ball from left to right in which the handle of the stick is first spun one half turn, bringing the flat side of the blade into a hitting position behind the ball.

SCOOP—A shoveling type of stroke in which the ball is lifted high into the air.

SHOOTING CIRCLE—*See* Striking circle.

SHORT CORNER—A free hit that is awarded a member of the attacking team when a defensive player commits a foul inside the striking circle. Also called penalty corner.

16-YARD HIT OUT—The free hit awarded a member of the defensive team when the attacking team causes the ball to go out of bounds over the goal line. The ball is placed down 16 yards from the goal line and at a point opposite where the ball went out of bounds.

STRIKING CIRCLE—The nearly semicircular area in front of each goal. A goal can occur only when the ball is hit from within the striking circle. Also called shooting circle.

TACKLE—To knock the ball away from an opponent's stick.

U.S. FIELD HOCKEY ASSOCIATION—The governing body of women's field hockey in the United States.

WING—A forward who is stationed on the outside of the forward line, close to the sideline.